PS   Wright, C. D.
3573
.R497   String light.
S77
1991

$18.00

DATE			

LITERATURE & LANGUAGE DEPT.
CHICAGO PUBLIC LIBRARY
400 SOUTH STATE STREET
CHICAGO, IL 60605

© THE BAKER & TAYLOR CO.

STRING LIGHT

STRING LIGHT

Poems by

C.D. WRIGHT

The University of Georgia Press
Athens and London

© 1991 by C. D. Wright
Published by the University of Georgia Press
Athens, Georgia 30602
All rights reserved
Designed by Betty Palmer McDaniel
Set in Stempel Garamond with Huxley Vertical display
The paper in this book meets the guidelines for
permanence and durability of the Committee on
Production Guidelines for Book Longevity of the
Council on Library Resources.

Printed in the United States of America

95 94 93 92 91   5 4 3 2 1

Library of Congress Cataloging in Publication Data

Wright, C. D.
String light : poems / by C. D. Wright.
p. cm.
ISBN 0-8203-1297-5 (alk. paper). — ISBN 0-8203-1298-3
(pbk. : alk. paper)
I. Title.
PS3573.R497S77   1991
811'.54—dc20   90-45957
CIP

British Library Cataloging in Publication Data available

for Ruth and Walter

If I were not human I would not be ashamed of anything.
W. S. MERWIN

Acknowledgments

Grateful acknowledgment is due to the following publications in which some of these poems or versions thereof originally appeared:

Caliban: "Personals"
Denver Quarterly: "The Night I Met Little Floyd," "The Ozark Odes," "The Next Time I Crossed the Line into Oklahoma"
Epoch: "Narrativity Scenes," "Humidity"
Field: "Planks," "Mons Venus," "Self Portrait on a Rocky Mount"
Five Fingers Review: "Utopia"
Ironwood: "Why Ralph Refuses to Dance"
Kenyon Review: "The box this comes in"
Organica: "The Next to Last Draft"
The Paris Review: "More Blues and the Abstract Truth," "Our Dust"
The Pennsylvania Review: "Remarks on Colour," "The Body's Temperature at Rest"
Poetry East: "Weekend in the Country"
raccoon: "King's Daughters, Home for Unwed Mothers, 1948"
Sulfur: "What No One Could Have Told Them," "Detail from *What No One Could Have Told Them*"

I would also like to thank the John Simon Guggenheim Memorial Foundation and the Mary Ingraham Bunting Institute at Radcliffe College for fellowships which were a great help during the period in which these poems were written.

The publication of this book is supported by a grant
from the National Endowment for the Arts,
a federal agency.

Contents

I
Mons Venus 3
King's Daughters, Home for Unwed Mothers, 1948 4
Narrativity Scenes 6
More Blues and the Abstract Truth 8
Remarks on Colour 10
The Night I Met Little Floyd 12
Why Ralph Refuses to Dance 14
Our Dust 16
Trends of Contemporary Living
and Problems That Demand Solution 19
Humidity 21

II
The Body's Temperature at Rest 25
The Next Time I Crossed the Line into Oklahoma 27
Personals 29
Planks 30
Utopia 32
Toward the Woods 34
What No One Could Have Told Them 36
Detail from *What No One Could Have Told Them* 39
Additional Detail . . . 40
Old Man with a Dog 41
Living 42
Weekend in the Country 45

III

The Next to Last Draft 51
Self Portrait on a Rocky Mount 53
The Ozark Odes 54
The box this comes in 59

STRING LIGHT

Lake Return

Maybe you have to be from there to hear it sing:
Give me your water weeds, your nipples,
your shoehorns and four-year letter jackets,
the molded leftovers from the singed pot.
Now let me see your underside, white as fishes.
I lower my gaze against your clitoral light.

Mons Venus

The train makes frightening time. Passengers dream their shirts undone.
It screams toward the lake. The salt box houses shake
their contents at a morning.
In a few minutes we can see the black dog asleep
in the marigolds, the widow on her three-pronged cane
poling to the convenience store; the first shift
jawing around at the coffee machine. For now
we drowse in a closet of light. Absently pull at the hair
under our gown. Jostle a hanger from a uniform. The old place
where we were born raises a rambunctious new clan.
We are the single women: we work to support our cars.
We come home to a good robe, a loofah for the backbone.
It's a short walk to the water from the tracks.
No one mans the caboose. Whatever the weather,
the pulp mills smell like bodies rotting in rain.
If we put our foot in childhood's shoe, the smell stays the same.
Who could count the animals we've swerved to avoid
or particles of sand scrubbed from our cracks.
Just sharing a smoke at the store before we punch in,
driving along the shore with the sun and radio waves
makes us want to kiss our arms and let the wind at our underwear
while the rooms we left to the cat turn optical. The train slackens
beyond traces of its scream. Passengers let up their shade, missing the lake.

King's Daughters, Home for Unwed Mothers, 1948

Somewhere there figures a man. In uniform. He's not white. He
could be AWOL. Sitting on a mattress riddled with cigarette burns.
Night of a big game in the capital. Big snow.
Beyond Pearl River past Petal and Leaf River and Macedonia;
it is a three-storied house. The only hill around. White.
The house and hill are white. Lighted upstairs, down.
She is up on her elbows, bangs wet and in her eyes. The head
of the unborn is visible at the opening. The head
crowns. Many helping hands are on her. She is told not to push.
But breathe. A firm voice.
With helping hands. They open the howl of her love. Out of her issues:

volumes of letters, morning glories on a string trellis, the job at the
Maybelline Factory, the job at the weapons plant, the hummingbird
hive, her hollyhocks, her grandmother's rigid back next to her
grandfather's bow, the briefest reflection of her mother's braid falling
below her wing blades, her atomizers and silverbacked brush and comb,
the steel balls under her father's knuckles, the moon's punched-out face,
his two-dollar neckties, the peacock coming down the drive; there was
the boy shuffling her way with the melon on his shoulder, car dust all
over his light clothes, the Black Cat fireworks sign on the barn, her
father's death from moving the barn by himself, the family sitting in the
darkened room drinking ice tea after the funeral, tires blown out on the
macadam, the women beaten like eggs, the store with foundation
garments, and boys pelting the girls with peony buds, the meatgrinder
cringing in the corner of the store, the old icebox she couldn't fix and
couldn't sell so buried to keep out the kids, her grandmother's pride, the
prettiest lavalier, the pole houses; there was the boy with the melon
shifted to the other shoulder, coming her way, grown taller and darker,
wiping his sweat with his hand, his beautiful Nubian head, older and set

upon by the longingly necked girls from the bottoms, his fishing hole,
learning the equations of equality: six for the white man and none for
the rest; the sloping shadows and blue hollows behind his shack, what
the sunflowers saw, the wide skirts she wore, the lizards they caught, the
eagerness with which they went through each other's folds of hair and
skin, the boy's outnumbered pride. . . .

This couldn't go on, the difficulty of concealment, putting make-up
over a passion mark. 1947, summer of whiskey and victory and
fear. It was long, then over. The letters burned. She heaves. Bleeds.
In the words of the grandmother: Do not eat oranges under the moon,
eat fruit that is green and cold. What was meant by that, really.
The infant's head is huge. She tears. He's white. He'll make it
just fine. The firm voice. The hands that helped.
What would become of this boychild. The uniformed man and she
will never know. That they will outlive him. They will never know.
That he will do things they never dreamed.

Narrativity Scenes

Six o'clock. Dark planing light.
I wonder where the gravedigger Valentino
Curly is holing up; Blue Cloud Wright,
slaughterhouse worker. This is the night
before Christmas, couples are fighting in cars
on every major highway in the country.
I lean against my door, mad again. This is the night . . .
I see myself stepping off a curb
in Kansas City after a little bowl
of eggdrop soup. Then we're in Sanborns,
Mexico, D.F., perusing the paper. We look
into our spoons, then it's the exhaust of a bus
with signs on the rear cautioning
Christians Under Construction.
Now I want to head home and crawl
under the bed. This is the night . . .
Umpteen years ago when I was a glittering green
elf, along with the Fletcher boys
in the Christmas parade. We rode with Santa,
the real one, in a white Thunderbird
loaned for the occasion. Mother drove.
First time on power brakes. At the light
she threw one Fletcher to the dash. Broke his tooth
or was it the nose. One Fletcher made a geologist.
That's how we said it, So and so made
a doctor. So and so made a rock hound.
The eldest shipped to Vietnam. Shipped back
in a metal chair. He lived, I was told,
in the woods collecting lugers, daggers, helmets.
He drank and drove himself into a tree. At the light . . .
I was named for his mother, I am told. Valentino

Curly put him down. At the light.
Blue Cloud has no bearing on this account.
It's the night before Christmas.
I was thinking about him. And someone else,
somebody I haven't seen in a while
sent me this book *Cooking for One*.
Now we are two. Soon to be more.
How will we manage. Life can be so sour.
At the light. I'll milk while you paint.
You milk while I paint. Who o who
is willing and eager to hold the baby
while we go up the ladder?
Yonder where the light is planing the dark.

More Blues and the Abstract Truth

I back the car over a soft, large object;
hair appears on my chest in dreams.
The paper boy comes to collect
with a pitbull. Call Grandmother
and she says, Well you know
death is death and none other.

In the mornings we're in the dark;
even at the end of June
the zucchini keep on the sill.
Ring Grandmother for advice
and she says, O you know
I used to grow so many things.

Then there's the frequent bleeding,
the tender nipples and the rot
under the floormat. If I'm not seeing
a cold-eyed doctor it is
another gouging mechanic.
Grandmother says, Thanks to the blue rugs
and Eileen Briscoe's elms
the house keeps cool.

Well. Then. You say Grandmother
let me just ask you this:
How does a body rise again and rinse
her mouth from the tap. And how
does a body put in a plum tree
or lie again on top of another body
or string a trellis. Or go on drying
the flatware. Fix rainbow trout. Grout the tile.

Buy a bag of onions. Beat an egg stiff. Yes,
how does the cat continue
to lick itself from toenail to tailhole.
And how does a body break
bread with the word when the word
has broken. Again. And. Again.
With the wine. And the loaf.
And the excellent glass
of the body. And she says,

Even. If. The. Sky. Is. Falling.
My. Peace. Rose. Is. In. Bloom.

Remarks on Colour

1. highway patched with blacktop, service station at the crossroads
2. creme soda in the popbox, man sitting on the popbox
3. a fully grown man
4. filthy toilets, just hold it a little while longer
5. shacks ringed with day lilies, then a columned house in shade
6. condensation off the soybeans
7. someone known as Skeeter
8. his whole life
9. flatbed loaded with strip-ed melons
10. Lopez's white car at JB's mother's house
11. katydids crepitating in the tall grass
12. gar wrapping itself in your line
13. gourds strung between poles
14. imagine a tribe of colour-blind people, and there could easily be one, they would not have the same colour concepts as we do
15. that's trumpet vine; that's what we call potato vine
16. no potatoes come of it though
17. no potatoes I know
18. I come back here about three years ago to see if I could eke out a living then I run onto Rhonda
19. help me Rhonda help help me Rhonda
20. E-Z on E-Z off
21. out of wedlock, wedlocked
22. planks nailed across kitchen doorway for a bar; living room turned into dance floor
23. drinking canned heat
24. the shit can make you permanently blind
25. sizzling nights
26. what do you suppose became of Fontella Bass
27. get your own sound then notes go with your sound—it's like a colour, my colour—I'm black brown with a little red-orange in my skin;

28. red looks good on me
29. and yet we could imagine circumstances under which we would say, these people see other colours in addition to ours
30. what the Swede concluded; if you want to know what's the matter with blacks in America study the other side of the colour line
31. I am just telling you what the man figured out
32. there is, after all, no commonly accepted criterion for what is a colour unless it is one of our colours
33. check this:
34. at the time of his death Presley's was the second most reproduced image in the world
35. the first was Mickey Mouse
36. Lansky Brothers—down on Beale—outfitted the johns of Memphis
37. and Elvis
38. R-U ready for Jesus R-U packed up
39. just don't compare me to any white musicians
40. the symphony they got seventy guys all playing one note
41. take me witcha man when you go

The Night I Met Little Floyd

a Friday or he would not have come to town—he would have
been working in the hills—Esmerelda and the cowboys let Jessie
and me off in front of the duplex—where I lived with
Sonnyman—Little Floyd was in my front room with a book in
his lap—coming back from Tulsa—I did the driving—stripping
gears—we lurched forward—Little Floyd rocked back and
forth in my chair—under the three-way lamp—in Tulsa Jessie
had an abortion—she lay in a coil on the lining of her coat—the
truck groaned on—we stopped for Chinese food—I insisted we
stop—eat—while we were in Tulsa—Jessie was cold—didn't
want to be in a booth—eating Chinese food under fluorescent
tubing—after her abortion—she wanted to go home to her own
hot water bottle—feel warmer—smaller—looked after—the
way in church her grandmother's hand used to pet her
incredible hair—offer her half a stick of chewing gum to
quieten her—while the pastor raised Cain—Little Floyd was
big—full-bearded—once in a while he crossed or uncrossed his
sockfeet—a big man reading in a little pool of light—his
hillbilly face absorbed—Jessie cold—in my rocking chair under
the three-way lamp—in the duplex—the truck broke down—
Jessie and I left it hulking beside the road in the brown grass—
under Oklahoma's brown sky—banged the doors and walked—
Little Floyd was Sonnyman's friend—it wasn't long before a
fast loud car came along—skidding to a stop—we squalled
off—with Esmerelda—blasted—and her lap dog—perpetually
runny-eyed—she was going to Arkansas—just one short stop to
make—a farm—not a bit out of the way—to see her
boyfriends—pretty albino boys with albino ponytails—both so
good—not to mention their undulant fields of alfalfa—dense
woods of marijuana—she could not choose—I don't know
another thing about people in Oklahoma—we waited around
for them to cross the line into Arkansas—for the big Friday

night drunk—which is the real reason Little Floyd was in town—but he got sidetracked by a book—Sonnyman loaned him a key—this had to be a Friday—Jessie coiled up in her cold—Sonnyman gone—the cat rubbing Little Floyd's sockfeet—in the brothers' farmhouse—a despondent couch—three lame chairs—stereo—a no-good television—woodstove—everyone but Jessie standing by the kitchen oven smoking—blasted—she wanted to be home—be warmer—smaller—looked after—at last one brother picked up his hat—we were close to the line—Esmerelda and the cowboys let us off in front of the duplex—we could see through the visqueen—the man rocking in the lighted room—a book in his lap—the cat arranging herself across the fly of his jeans—Sonny's friend—reading *Ladies from Hell*—in two years Sonnyman would be dead—in a few more years Jessie's boyfriend died too—the truck belonged to him—Little Floyd keeps coming in from the hills on Friday—closes the bars—if I leave the key in the spider plant he falls out on the floor—snores until late on Saturday—takes me out to breakfast—Jessie moved—she fell into a dark shaft of money—married a sweet east Texas man—the truck remained on the side of the road a week or so—Jessie's landlord crossed the line into Oklahoma with chains—and dragged its chassis back to Arkansas—maybe we didn't have enough good times—not enough times when someone jumped up and said—let's float the Buffalo—take off for the river with a borrowed canoe—come back the next evening—dirty dishes still on the table—we tended to wait around until we were left by the hellbent whiskered men with their indelible smells—our sorry shoes huddled together by the bed—Oklahoma was a stand of trees without leaves—brown grass brown sky—weathervanes sharp and thin as women blown this way and that—cold beef suppers—3.2 beer—Arkansas—a pot of lentils and bad coffee—rocking chairs—three-way lamps—night running down our face like mascara—a big bearded stranger with a book of poems in his lap

Why Ralph Refuses to Dance

He would have to put out his smoke.
  At this time of year the snakes are slow and sorry-acting
His ice would melt. He'd lose his seat.
  you don't take chances once in a while you still see
He does not feel the beat.
  a coontail tied to an aerial, but don't look
His pocket could be picked. His trousers rip.
  for signs keep your black shoes on the floor
He could break a major bone.
  burn every tick you pull off your head
He remembers the last time he stepped out on the floor.
  roll a set of steel balls around in your fist
Who do you think I am, she said, a broom.
  looking at the moon's punched-out face
No, he mumbled, saxophone.
  think about Lily coming down the staircase
At the tables they whispered about him.
  her crushed velvet chairs
He would begin to smell of baby shrimp.
  her pearled brown toes
The music could stop in the middle of his action.
  that time with the three of them in a boat
What would he do with his hands.
  and him throwing up in the river
The women his age are spoken for.
  as she stood up to skim his hat into the shallows
After sitting out so long, his heart could give out.
  and tomorrow would unleash another spell of spare-rib theology
People will be stepped on. A fight ensue.
  aw shuddup somebody clapped a hand on his shoulder

The cats in the band will lose respect.
   aw shuddup he was getting the heavy hand again
He will bring dishonor to his family name.
   are you going to dance or not, just say
good night, no thanks, hallelujah yourself, go to hell.

Our Dust

I am your ancestor. You know next-to-nothing
about me.
There is no reason for you to imagine
the rooms I occupied or my heavy hair.
Not the faint vinegar smell of me. Or
the rubbered damp
of Forrest and I coupling on the landing
en route to our detached day.

You didn't know my weariness, error, incapacity.
I was the poet
of shadow work and towns with quarter-inch
phone books, of failed
roadside zoos. The poet of yard eggs and
sharpening shops,
jobs at the weapons plant and the Maybelline
factory on the penitentiary road.

A poet of spiderwort and jacks-in-the-pulpit,
hollyhocks against the tool shed.
An unsmiling dark blond.
The one with the trowel in her handbag.
I dug up protected and private things.
That sort, I was.
My graves went undecorated and my churches
abandoned. This wasn't planned, but practice.

I was the poet of shorttailed cats and yellow
line paint.
Of satellite dishes and Peterbilt trucks. Red Man
Chewing Tobacco, Triple Hit

Creme Soda. Also of dirt daubers nightcrawlers,
martin houses, honey, and whetstones
from the Novaculite Uplift. What remained
of The Uplift.

I had registered dogs 4 sale; rocks, dung
and straw.
I was a poet of hummingbird hives along with
redheaded stepbrothers.

The poet of good walking shoes—a necessity
in vernacular parts—and push mowers.
The rumor that I was once seen sleeping
in a refrigerator box is false (he was a brother
who hated me).
Nor was I the one lunching at the Governor's
mansion.

I didn't work off a grid. Or prime the surface
if I could get off without it. I made
simple music
out of sticks and string. On side B of me,
experimental guitar, night repairs and suppers
such as this.
You could count on me to make a bad situation
worse like putting liquid make-up over
a passion mark.

I never raised your rent. Or anyone else's by God.
Never said I loved you. The future gave me chills.
I used the medium to say: Arise arise and
come together.
Free your children. Come on everybody. Let's start
with Baltimore.

Believe me I am not being modest when I
admit my life doesn't bear repeating. I
agreed to be the poet of one life,
one death alone. I have seen myself
in the black car. I have seen the retreat
of the black car.

Trends of Contemporary Living and Problems That Demand Solution

Harmon and Nan are driving over Crowley's ridge looking for Nan's cat. Some animal is spotted ahead. Grey fur. Harmon parks and walks to its body. Before he finds a rock, the wheezing stops. He comes back and turns the car around. Was that Sister, she asks. No, he tells her, possum.

During an electrical storm a hundred-year-old pinoak fell on their living room. This winter the yard took on an unfortunate symmetry.

Your wife is a wonder, the druggist brags when Harmon goes to have a prescription filled. I know she is, he smiles. And for a surge of brainless seconds, he suspects the druggist whom he has known for many years.

Harmon has topsoil trucked in, and railroad ties to bank his tomato bed. He binds them to stakes with stockings. Nan doesn't look forward to canning the yield. When she sees him curve over his trowel she draws the curtains to search for a bottle he could have overlooked.

Sister traps a finch low in the lilac bush. Harmon, a lover of fowl, turns the hose hard on the Persian. Nan raps the porch window with her heavily ringed fist.

His: ragged undershorts, auction boxes, belching, dandruff, scratching, profanity, bad cooking.

Her: crosswords, unfinished knitting, drinking, dead plants, clammy skin, spoiled cat, bad cooking.

They met under a bridge spanning a green river. The day was hot and clear. He kept pulling in a turtle. Seven rainbow trout quivered on her stringer. Her back was freckled and he could see her vertebrae. He wore his hat at an appealing angle. The bridge was built by the WPA. Nan's favorite brother worked for the WPA. It was the best job he ever had.

Humidity

There are no houses no trees there is no body
    of water. Things are as they seem.
They are driving around another beltway of light.
A hand glows under the radio's green dial.
Both are taken up with their own itinerant thoughts
about the borrowed binoculars or mineral rights
to an unknown relative's land. They are at a point in space
where animate dark meets inanimate darkness.
Flares from refineries ignite their faces.
    There are no houses no trees. . . .
Pods of satellite dishes focus on an unstable sky.
Soon they will exit and look for a cafe
where there are people. We'll hear them order
charcoal and beer, watching the fan work the smoke.
They could even take a room, and submit
unto the soaked bedding with one hundred strokes of night.
Here where imperfection gives way to perfection;
there are no houses no trees and no body of water.
    Things are as they seem.

The Body's Temperature at Rest

While you are walking across the Orient
in a yellow paisley shirt,
I go around the house
killing flies the rain drove indoors.

I sit in the shade drinking ice water
When I bend to pick up paper against the fence
it blows into brown stalks of the cosmos;
I can feel you leaning back on your heels
chewing on the good times and the bad.

Mornings I dip a cold biscuit in the black coffee
and look out at the new shoots.
Before the tower blinks into view
I'm up on the step in my pajamas caressing the cat.
It's only Tuesday, we both have our heads in our paws.

When night gets here the wind
whips the breath out of the bushes
and there is nothing more to do
but go inside and shut the door.

Sometimes I touch the mirror in the dark
and think of the cold noses of my brother's dogs
or seeing myself flicker against the shadowed walls
I'm reminded of the Villines' boy
trying to kiss my eleven-year-old lips.
Not much stirs on our block at this hour
unless a coarse hand brushes over some coarse hair.

I've been sleeping with all the pillows
in the house and a lead pipe. Doors bang.
By the tired light I read
The Rise and Fall of the Third Reich.
The same car rumbles around the block.

Since her wires were cut, the old
Republican next door doesn't budge
from her brick fort but under escort
in a heavy car. The mulberry threatens
the fence. The dark-complected girl behind us,
she's gone completely wild this June.

I imagine you there
standing among 100,000 irises;
here, where the beds have died back
and you are always up before me
with your face and genitals washed
seated at your desk with a straight spine,
a clear head—writing another version
in which the irises are spreading.

If you come looking for me
and I'm not knocking dirt daubers out of the rafters
or watching re-runs over a light supper,
come down to the pond; nab another bottle
of Mateus. When it's cool like this
I sit on a log under your poncho
burping back at the frogs.

The Next Time I Crossed the Line into Oklahoma

we borrowed Little Floyd's car—he got held up dehorning trees—Jessie and I left early—making a run to see Esmerelda—and buy a lid of homegrown—Little Floyd handed over the keys—Jessie and I waited until he was long gone in his pick-up before we turned the motor over—the car jumped back—Little Floyd would be revving his chainsaw among the dead limbs and power lines—the car lurched forward—Little Floyd was a big full-bearded hillbilly—everyone remarked it was a wonder—how he skinnied up a tree like a cat—we made it over there with no snags—Esmerelda's house was empty—curtains aflutter with hot air—farm kittens licked down in their fur—cowboys gave us directions to Indians—Indians gave us directions to cowboys—poker games going on in front rooms—we were drinking 3.2 like well water—none more skillful than Little Floyd—when it came to clearing live wire and felling redhearts—when it came to saving sick elm he was the only one—how one dirt road led to another—finally we ended up at the right one—Esmerelda's loud car parked among the pick-ups—poker in the front room—a blanket blocking off the next room—one cowboy went in—one Indian came out—who's to say why in Oklahoma there is silence—while in Arkansas everyone jumps in everyone else's business—a low loving moan unfurled from the backside of the blanket—Jessie's nails sprang into my forearm—we scrambled into the same door behind the wheel—we were both driving—until we reached the line we didn't talk about going to get Esmerelda—then we talked about going to get Esmerelda non-stop while we tore home—Jessie rolled down the window puking—before we ground the Impala into park right in front of the duplex—the one where

Sonnyman was to blow out his lights—another nightmare in the works—we coasted through the carwash—Little Floyd was ready to throw a rod—he didn't ask if we scored the homegrown

Personals

Some nights I sleep with my dress on. My teeth
are small and even. I don't get headaches.
Since 1971 or before, I have hunted a bench
where I could eat my pimento cheese in peace.
If this were Tennessee and across that river, Arkansas,
I'd meet you in West Memphis tonight. We could
have a big time. Danger, shoulder soft.
Do not lie or lean on me. I am still trying to find a job
for which a simple machine isn't better suited.
I've seen people die of money. Look at Admiral Benbow. I wish
like certain fishes, we came equipped with light organs.
Which reminds me of a little known fact:
if we were going the speed of light, this dome
would be shrinking while we were gaining weight.
Isn't the road crooked and steep.
In this humidity, I make repairs by night. I'm not one
among millions who saw Monroe's face
in the moon. I go blank looking at that face.
If I could afford it I'd live in hotels. I won awards
in spelling and the Australian crawl. Long long ago.
Grandmother married a man named Ivan. The men called him
Eve. Stranger, to tell the truth, in dog years I am up there.

Planks

While we are all together under burring bulbs we would do well
to remember the wild rose in the pelvis bone. Albumen.
The accoutrements and utensils of love. And labor.
A soft robe. A solid teapot. Our talking guitar.
Why not go to a green field. Barefooted, hair unbound. And fill
our belly with short sweet grass. Cover the shorn shoulders
with new wool. Rid the body of its white implacability.
Bite down and hold on. Remember string light.

Remember lives on the periphery: the Indian in handcuffs.
The twin sisters who man the mausoleum. Or just standing in line
we could shut our eyes. Stop counting. Imagine:
the color Naomi Trosper wanted to paint West Memphis;
now picture West Memphis, gentian violet.
While we are starching our coats for their steel constructions
we could be shining the particulars; emery boards,
grasshoppers . . . , remembering the birth of our boy. The giant hibiscus.

The first feces, meconium. Forever bearing in mind why
we have been assembled. Remember pain. The night Yolanda lost her baby.
Bite down and hold on. Be ourselves chastened,
doing away with engraved gifts, boxes of miscellany.
Ignore the butcherbirds. The aims of the ruthless. Bad endings.
Breakfasts of Coca Cola and cigarette smoke. Sabotage. Stay
down and let go. Of vain love. The frayed light. All together now.
The night Esmerelda came to town and laid an egg. Forget pain.

Alone and awake in our cells like a bird left without a blanket,
we would do well to find the wild rose in the pelvis bone; turn
our back on the figure in the undergrowth, the felo-de-se,
his draining face. Albumen. Let us go back to the green field. And lie down.

Eliminate strategies. The key to the handcuffs. Singing nail file. Acridadae. Bury Yolanda's placenta. The pain. Esmerelda's egg. The pain Naomi's violet city. Childbirth. Our talking guitar. We must bite down and hold on. Never mind learning to draw. The giant hibiscus.

Utopia

Inside of me
there are no cathedrals
even in the vaulted halls
where you thought you would come upon
some providential soul
letting go a cage of doves
there are only vaulted halls.

Inside of me
there is a period of mud,
flies and midges come with the mud
followed by a time of intense sun;
with the sun comes a cool room
furnished by a rotating fan, a typing machine.
While there is sun I type then I walk
often for long stretches
in search of hidden springs, curative herbs
or not in search of a blessed thing.

Inside of me
a stranger rubs its knees
against the palings of my ribs
someone who may be born to fail,
a drifter hunched over a cinder block
pitching rock at mounds of garbage,
someone who may catch and tear
like a plastic bag in a fence.

But beyond this zone
of tire heaps and oil drums
a clearing entertains one tree;

where you thought you would come upon
blades of steel light or where
you thought the doves would collect themselves
there is only enough soil enough blood
and seed good enough for one tree.

Toward the Woods

The ones who were there stood
at the ends of the body.

Afterwards
I was pronounced dead.

I was sore with cold.
Nothing was marked up or down.

On the way out of a dense white woods
I composed matchbook odes.

I dropped crumbs of fresh paper,
passed a woman who seemed to know

something about where I had come from.
"I talked to Arkansas last night," she says.

"It's 80 degrees there," she adds. Friendly.
"They had thunderstorms all week."

I was feeling better. Looking
suddenly forward to the unpondered night.

Before the trees closed in on me
I watched two boys fighting by the river.

First I wanted the featherweight
then the freckled one.

And I glimpsed the bottom
of my husband's long-nailed toes

as he flopped
off the bank like a gator.

Ah, there he is now, Forrest,
in the ultra-silent light of a new kitchen

sitting across from our son
who has at last outgrown his cradle cap.

They have arranged themselves
at a strangely shaped table,

and appear to be sharing
a mold of frozen food.

They are draped in a sarong or toga
their penises scored with age.

What No One Could Have Told Them

Once he comes to live on the outside of her, he will not sleep through the night or the next 400. He sleeps not, they sleep not. Ergo they steer gradually mad. The dog's head shifts to another paw under the desk. Over a period of 400 nights.

You will see, she warns him. Life is full of television sets, invoices, organs of other animals thawing on counters.

In her first dream of him, she leaves him sleeping on Mamo's salt bag quilt behind her alma mater. Leaves him to the Golden Goblins. Sleep, pretty one, sleep.

. . . *the quilt that comforted her brother's youthful bed, the quilt he took to band camp.*

Huh oh, he says, Huh oh. His word for many months. Merrily pouring a bottle of Pledge over the dog's dull coat. And with a round little belly that shakes like jelly.

Waiting out a shower in the Border Cafe, the bartender spoons a frozen strawberry into his palm leaf basket while they lift their frosted mugs in a grateful click.

He sits up tall in his grandfather's lap, waving and waving to the Blue Bonnet truck. Bye, blue, bye.

In the next dream he stands on his toes, executes a flawless flip onto the braided rug. Re-springs to crib.

The salt bag quilt goes everywhere, the one the bitch Rosemary bore her litters on. The one they wrap around the mower, and bundle with black oak leaves.

How the bowl of Quick Quaker Oats fits his head.

He will have her milk at 1:42, 3:26, 4 a.m. Again at 6. Bent over the rail to settle his battling limbs down for an afternoon nap. Eyes shut, trying to picture what in the world she has on.

His nightlight—a snowwhite pair of porcelain owls.

They remember him toothless, with one tooth, two tooths, five or seven scattered around in his head. They can see the day when he throws open his jaw to display several vicious rows.

Naked in a splash of sun, he pees into a paper plate the guest set down in the grass as she reached for potato chips.

Suppertime, the dog takes leave of the desk's cool cavity to patrol his highchair.

How patiently he pulls Kleenex from a box. Tissue by tissue. How quietly he stands at the door trailing the White Cloud; swabs his young hair with the toilet brush.

The dog inherits the salt bag quilt. The one her Mamo made when she was seventeen—girlfriends stationed around a frame in black stockings sewing, talking about things their children would do;

He says: cereal, byebye, shoe, raisin, nobody. He hums.

She stands before the medicine chest, drawn. Swiftly he tumps discarded tampax and hair from an old comb into her tub.

Wearily the man enters the house through the back. She isn't dressed. At the table there is weeping. Curses. Forking dried breasts of chicken.

while Little Sneed sat on the floor beneath the frame, pushing the needles back through.

One yawn followed by another yawn. Then little fists screwing little eyes. The wooden crib stuffed with bears and wind-up pillows wheeled in to receive him. Out in a twinkle. The powdered bottom airing the dark. The 400th night. When they give up their last honeyed morsel of love; the dog nestles in the batting of the salt bag quilt commencing its long mope to the death.

Detail from *What No One Could Have Told Them*

Naked in a splash of sun, he pees into a paper plate
the guest set down on the lawn as she reached
naked in a splash of sun into a naked sun splash
He pees naked into a paper plate a plate the guest set down
into a plate of white paper the guest set down He pees
into a plate the guest set down on the lawn in back of the airy house
a paper plate the guest set down He pees on the lawn
He pees into a white paper plate a living fountain of pee
a golden jet of pure baby pee from His seven month old penis
His uncircumcised penis not even one year old a jet
of pure gold into an uncircumcised splash of sun
a beautiful gold arc of pee in a splash of uncircumcised sun
naked in a splash of sun He pees into a paper plate
a white paper plate the guest set down on the airy lawn
in back of the airy white house into a paper white plate
weighted down with baked beans and slabs of spiced ham
the guest set down on the lawn in back of the white house
on the lovely expanse of lawn the guest set down the paper plate
on the lawn as she leaned forward in the canvas sling
of her chair as she reached out of her green sleeve
into a white paper plate the guest set down on the lawn He pees
as she reached out of her green butterfly sleeve
out of the beautiful arc of her iridescent sleeve as she
set down on the expanding lovely lawn a paper plate
He pees naked in a splash of sun as she reached for potato chips.

Additional Detail . . .

One yawn followed by another then little fists screwing little eyes one yawn followed by little fists screwing another yawn followed by little eyes followed by one little yawn followed by fists followed by another little yawn screwing eyes out in a twinkle another yawn followed by little fists screwing eyes out in a little twinkle followed by the powdered bottom airing the dark twinkle followed by another yawn out in a twinkle little fists screwing little eyes then another yawn followed by a twinkle then another yawn in a twinkle followed by the powdered bottom airing the dark yawn followed by little fists screwing eyes out in a little twinkle followed by another powdered bottom airing the dark yawn followed by another dark bottom when they give up airing the dark powdered by another yawn when they give up the bottom then another yawn followed by little fists powdering their last yawn when they give up another yawn followed by their last honeyed morsel then little fists screwing another yawn followed by little eyes out in a twinkle followed by the powdered bottom airing the dark then another yawn then little fists when they give up screwing the dark when they give up their last honeyed morsel another yawn then little eyes out in a twinkle followed by the powdered bottom airing the dark when they give up another yawn followed by their last honeyed morsel of love.

Old Man with a Dog

climbing the hill
in a heavy coat
to Sunset Manor
to comb his wife's
white clumps of hair,
muttering,
72 years,
what you cannot
end up with
in 72 years.
Eating at the stove
in his heavy coat.
Watching tv
with the dog.
72 years
on the heel of this
Christbitten hill.
72 years
he wonders aloud,
What will I do?
How will I live?

Living

If this is Wednesday, write Lazartigues, return library books, pick up passport form, cancel the paper.

If this is Wednesday, mail B her flyers and K her shirts. Last thing I asked as I walked K to her car, "You sure you have everything?" "Oh yes," she smiled, as she squalled off. Whole wardrobe in front closet.

Go to Morrison's for paint samples, that's where housepainter has account (near Pier One), swing by Gano St. for another bunch of hydroponic lettuce. Stop at cleaners if there's parking.

Pap smear at 4. After last month with B's ear infections, can't bear sitting in damn doctor's office. Never a magazine or picture on the wall worth looking at. Pack a book.

Ever since B born, nothing comes clear. My mind like a mirror that's been in a fire. Does this happen to the others.

If this is Wednesday, meet Moss at the house at noon. Pick B up first, call sitter about Friday evening. If she prefers, can bring B to her (hope she keeps the apartment warmer this year).

Need coat hooks and picture hangers for office. Should take car in for air filter, oil change. F said one of back tires low. Don't forget car payment, late last two months in a row.

If this is Wednesday, there's a demo on the green at 11. Took B to his first down at Quoinset Point in August. Blue skies. Boston collective provided good grub for all. Long column of denims and flannel shirts. Smell of Patchouli made me so wistful, wanted to buy a wood stove, prop my feet up, share a J and a pot of Constant Comment with a friend. Maybe some zucchini bread.

Meet with honors students from 1 to 4. At the community college I tried to incite them to poetry. Convince them this line of work, beat the bejesus out of a gig as gizzard splitter at the processing plant or cleaning up after a leak at the germ warfare center. Be all you can be, wrap a rubber band around your trigger finger until it drops off.

Don't forget to cancel the goddamned paper. At the very least quit reading editorials and police reports—local boys caught throwing sewer caps off the overpass again, not to mention recreational violence in the park next to our cashew-colored house every night of the year.

Swim at 10:00 before picking up B, before demo on the green, and before meeting Moss, if it isn't too crowded. Only three old women talking about their daughters-in-law last Wednesday at 10:00.

Phone hardware to see if radon test arrived.

Keep an eye out for a new yellow blanket. Left B's on the plane, though he seems over it already. Left most recent issue of Z in the seat. That will make a few businessmen boil. I liked the man who sat next to me, he was sweet to B. Hated flying, said he never let all of his weight down.

Need to get books in the mail today. Make time pass in line at the p.o. imagining man in front of me butt naked. Fellow in the good-preacher-blue suit, probably has a cold, hard bottom.

Call N for green tomato recipe. Have to get used to the yankee growing season. If this is Wednesday, N goes in hospital today. Find out how long after marrow transplant before can visit.

Mother said she read in paper that Pete was granted a divorce. His third. My highschool boyfriend. Meanest thing I could have done, I did to him, returning the long-saved-for engagement ring in a band-aid box, while he was stationed in Danang.

Meant to tell F this morning about dream of eating grasshoppers, fried but happy. Our love a difficult instrument we are learning to play. Practice, practice.

No matter where I call home anymore, feel like a boat under the trees. Living is strange.

This week only: bargain on laid paper at East Side Copy Shop.

Woman picking her nose at the stoplight. Shouldn't look, only privacy we have anymore in the car. Isn't that the woman from the colloquium last fall, who told me she was a stand-up environmentalist. What a wonderful trade, I said, because the evidence of planetary wrongdoing is overwhelming. Because because because of the horrible things we do.

If this is Wednesday, meet F at Health Department at 10:45 for AIDS test.

If this is Wednesday, it's trash night.

Weekend in the Country

How water is run
or
a hoover

a new hinge is put on the trunk
or
a screen tears

Machado is read
maybe

a jar breaks
or
a mirror

during an electrical storm
trees drop their fruit
or
some boards fall down

a walk with the 16 year old dog
or
a nap an apple a black and white tv

too much sun
or
shade

sitting in the yard after dark
a lightning bug in your hair
or
digging a hole for the dog

swim
or
avoid water and low wire

hanging the straw hat on a nail
or
throw it on the chair

cut your bangs
or
let your hair grow out

drive to town for liquor
and a movie
or
stay in for macaroni again

humming under the umbrella
en route to the mailbox
or
sleeping late

morning over a cantaloupe
and a day old paper
or
today's paper and no melon

another search
for the wristwatch
or
an address on a hardware bill

hearing things
or
a pot turns over on the porch

unexpected company
or
tipped back in a ladderback
watching ants
climb up your arm

|||

The Next to Last Draft

More years pass and the book does not leave the drawer. According to our author the book does not begin but opens on a typewriter near a radiator. The typing machine has been aimed at the window overlooking a park. It's been oiled and blown out. At heart it is domestic as an old washer with the white sheets coming off the platen. In the missing teeth much has been suppressed. In the space and a half, regrettable things have been said. Nothing can be taken back. The author wanted this book to be friendly, to say, Come up on the porch with me, I've got peaches; I don't mind if you smoke. It would be written in the author's own voice. A dedication was planned to Tyrone and Tina whose names the author read in a sidewalk on Broad. The machine's vocation was to type, but its avocation was to tell everyone up before light, I love you, I always will; to tell the sisters waiting on their amniocentesis, Everything's going to be fine. And to make something happen for the hundreds of Floridians betting the quinella. It would have dinner ready for people on their feet twelve hours a day. And something else for the ones making bread hand over fist, the gouging s-o-bs. But the book was too dependent. Women were scattered across pages who loved the desert, but moved into town to meet a man. The women, understand, weren't getting any younger. Some of these women were pecking notes into the text when the author was out walking. One note said: John Lee, you're still in my dreambooks, etcetera. The author had no foresight. In previous drafts the good died right off like notes on an acoustic guitar. Others died of money, that is, they fell of odorless, invisible, utterly quiet wounds. The work recorded whatever it heard: dog gnawing its rump, the stove's clock, man next door taking out his cans, and things that went on further down, below buildings and composts, all with the patience of a dumb beast chewing grass, with the inconsolable eyes of the herd. Basically the book was intended as a hair-raising document of the organisms. Thus and so the book opens: I have been meaning to write you for a long long time. I've been feeling so blue John Lee.

Self Portrait on a Rocky Mount

I am the goat. Caroline by name. Nee 6 January. Domesticated since the 6th century before Jesus, a goat himself.

We have served as a source of meat, leather, milk and hair. Our flesh is not widely loved. Yet our younger, under parts make fine gloves.

Out of our hair—pretty sweaters, wigs for magistrates. Our milk is good for cheese.

We share these gifts with Richard Milhous Nixon, who gained national prominence for his investigation of Mr. Hiss.

We're no sloth, full-time workers at the minimum wage, We had an annual income last year of $6,968, a little less than your average subway musician.

Our horoscope assures—we will be a great success socially and in some artistic calling.

We are sure-footed, esp. on hills. We live on next-to-nothing. This week's victuals: ironing board covers and swollen paperbacks. Our small hills of filings fall under the heading of useful by-products. This we call Industrial Poetry. Both of us being Bearded, Mystic, Horned.

The Ozark Odes

this one goes out to Fred

Lake Return

Maybe you have to be from there to hear it sing:
Give me your water weeds, your nipples,
your shoehorn and four-year letter jacket,
the molded leftovers from the singed pot.
Now let me see your underside, white as fishes.
I lower my gaze against your clitoral light.

Rent House

O the hours I lay on the bed
looking at the knotted pine
in the added-on room
where he kept his old Corona,
the poet with the big lips—
where we slept together.

Somebody's Mother

Flour rose from her shoulders
as she walked out of her kitchen.
The report of the screendoor,
the scrapdog unperturbed.
Afternoon sky pinking up.

Table Grace

Bless Lou Vindie, bless Truman,
Bless the fields
of rocks, the brown recluse
behind the wallpaper,

chink in the plaster,
bless cowchips, bless brambles
and the copperhead, the honey locusts
shedding their frilly flower
on waxed cars, bless them
the loudmouths and goiters
and dogs with the mange,
bless each and every one
for doing their utmost.
Yea, for they have done
their naturally suspicious part.

Girlhood

Mother had one. She and Bernice racing for the river
to play with their paperdolls
because they did not want any big ears
to hear what their paperdolls were fixing to say.

Judge

had a boyhood. Had his own rooster. Name of Andy.
Andy liked to ride in Judge's overall bib.
Made him bald. This really vexed Judge's old daddy.

Arkansas Towns

Acorn
Back Gate
Bald Knob
Ben Hur
Biggers
Blue Ball
Congo
Delight
Ebony

Eros
Fifty-Six
Figure Five
Flippin
Four Sisters
Goshen
Greasy Corner
Havana
Hector
Hogeye
Ink
Jenny Lind
Little Flock
Marked Tree
Mist
Monkey Run
Moscow
Nail
Okay
Ozone
Rag Town
Ratio
Seaton Dump
Self
Snowball
Snow Lake
Sweet Home
Three Brothers
Three Folks
Twist
Urbanette
Whisp
Yellville
Zent

Lake Return

Where the sharp rock on shore
give way to the hairy rock in the shallows.
we enlisted in the rise and fall of love.
His seed broadcast like short, sweet grass.
Nothing came up there.

Dry County Bar

Bourbon not fit to put on a sore. No women enter;
their men collect in every kind of weather
with no shirts on whatsoever.

Cafe at the Junction

The way she sees him
how the rain doesn't let up

4-ever blue and vigilant
as a clock in a corner

peeling the label from his bottle
hungry but not touching food

as she turns down the wet lane
where oaks vault the road

The Boyfriend

wakes in darkness of morning
and visits the water

lowering his glad body
onto a flat rock

the spiders rearrange
themselves underneath

Remedy

Sty sty leave my eye,
go to the next feller passing by.

Porch

I can still see Cuddihy's sisters
trimming the red tufts
under one another's arms.

Bait Shop

Total sales today: 3 dozen minnows, ½ doz crawdaddies, 4 lead lures,
loaf of light bread, pack of Raleighs, 3 bags of barbecued pork skins.

Fred

one of your more irascible poets from the hill country.
Retired to his mother's staunch house
in Little Rock after her death; began to build
a desk for Arthur. Beautiful piece
of work. For a friend. Beautiful.
Drinking less, putting on a few pounds.

Lake Return

Why I come here: need for a bottom, something to
    refer to;
where all things visible and invisible commence to swarm.

The box this comes in
(a deviation on poetry)

is not beautiful, at least it is not aggressively beautiful, meaning the workmanship, as it was formerly called—regardless of who took up the tools, but also generally reflecting to whom the tools were entrusted—falls on the faulty side, connoting the work shows: nail heads, blades which slipped past their mark in insuring the fit of the lid, steel screws securing brass hinges, and especially the irregular tooling of the conventionalized flowers. Though the flowers are suggestive of tulips and dogwoods, they are apt to be fleurs-de-lis and marvels-of-Peru. Because the work shows, I favor it more. It likewise follows, lacking mechanical perfection, the box was made by hand. Possibly for someone in particular rather than for sale. If the object was wages not affection, it was nevertheless made with the same two hands; practice rather than mastery guided its making. If true to tradition, the pay would have been unduly low; for motives ruled by affection the making would have been its own reward. The box was given to me by an old flame, now a virtually unbeaten trial lawyer. Flame is a hotter word than truthfully applies since we were bound by argument more than passion. In the end I was the wounded, but throughout I inflicted my rude, overbearing manner on him. Memories too keen to dwell upon. The first woman it was made or bought for has long occupied her own box. So does the maker—occupy a box of his own, that is if we follow the gender assumptions of the period in which it was made. On the other hand, the flowers are on the austere side, not overly feminine; perhaps it was meant to hold a man's effects. There is no loitering odor of cigars or of perfume. The wood is dark. The lining vanished but for the residual glue tracks and morsels of fabric attesting it was once faced with gold velvet. It measures $6\frac{7}{8}'' \times 11''$. The interior space offers an inch less in length and width, again to insure the lid's fit. The box stands 3″ tall.

Allow me to date it this way: the woman, whom I won't try to picture in detail, must have had a bundle of hair, as when it was bought for me 15 years ago, the dealer told my friend it was approximately 60 years old. Circa 1914. This would have been prior to the bob, a coif forbidden to this day according to an Arkansas statute. Little Rock is where it was bought but not where it necessarily originated. The antique dealers in that internal capital get around to wherever dealers in old things convene, and they venture out on their own: estate sales, flea markets, bank auctions. A dreamy novel could be written about the alleged maker and the alleged recipient, but merely to dream them up in period clothing, in love and trouble, does not stir me. I am more drawn to cold, factual things such as diet, income, fertility, abilities with animals, plants, interstellar links.

If I knew my woods once felled and fashioned, I would tell you what wood this is, what polish to apply. Generically, my guess is fruitwood, if this does not infer too gorgeous a grain. With trees in leaf or bloom, I am on a first name basis with an impressive number, even the paulownia, resembling the catalpa, which alongside the mimosa is treated as a nuisance tree in the little towns in the mountains as their frilly flowers damage car finish. Where cars are inviolable, totemic. The bodark remains my personal favorite—it being truly hard, burning blue in the fireplace and standing out by itself in a field with its extra half dozen monikers: hedge apple, horse apple, mock orange, osage orange, bow wood, bois d'arc, not to mention its bizarre globular fruit and lascivious smell. Diagonally across the lid stretches an ugly scar, unprofessionally repaired. The result of some lapse. Even from the underside the injury appears in reverse. The flowers which lace the lid and sides have been tipped with gold paint. Hopefully the painter did not wet the brushes with the inside of the mouth to bring them to a fine point in order to articulate the scrolling stems, because the odds are the pigment is tainted with a pretty poison.

The box holds a modest inventory of things kept in spite of their inverse relation to value: two bowties, one solid avocado green but patterned, one with lavender and pink diamonds on a purplish field (from my father's springy days). Three battery-operated watches, a strand of phony pearls, six or seven nondescript drugstore barrettes, one Italian butterfly clasp (for my sheared head). Clay beads from the Chrysler Museum shop in Norfolk, because they were a dollar and I was burning to buy something. Three flowered handkerchiefs from Mamo carefully folded inside her last birthday card to me—of the type she has carried in her handbag since she was a young woman to blot the lips, tamp the brow, blow the nose (although I can't for the life of me see myself blotting, tamping, much less blowing on them). One has been folded so as to bloom from a breast pocket. A black ribbon for an armband when the occasion calls (last donned Election Day). A strip of day-glo surveyor's tape pierced by an ordinary nail which belonged to Frank Stanford, poet, land surveyor. According to the late Stanford, the tape derives from a vegetable base, cows love it, causing the line just surveyed and flagged to vanish behind you. Also one notably odd handkerchief brought back for a souvenir of Seoul: short, parallel pink and aqua bars on a white cotton field surrounding a square frame which features a pig in a zoot suit. The pig stands in front of a tractor parked before a limelighted city. A poem inscribes the picture: "Listen, Can't you hear the Manhattan Blues? / Howdi? / Smoky Night. Moody shadow is behind my back. Slow ballad / is in my glass. Black trick is a sweet thing. City light is only my God." My notion of Seoul nights is undoubtedly as accurate as the Korean poet's of New York, New York. One fabric gardenia, misshapen and discolored. Three woven friendship bracelets, an enamel and pewter cross once on Frank Stanford's key chain. A silver dollar from Mamo, tin dragonfly from Jean Kondo, two frosted hair combs bought in a jewelry store in a small-town mall on the eve of my wedding. One star-shaped turquoise pin, one beaded leather ring I cannot remember borrowing or buying, neither of which I like even a little. Unstrung malachite beads. A lacquer poppy from the legionnaires.

The box maintains an honored place on my sewing machine bought at the sewing center on Broad Street because I imagined myself sewing, curved over yards of washable silk, giving the balance wheel a spin and treadling until the dress was done. Then I would put it on and go where, to the policeman's ball? "Howdi, Smoky Night." On my rickety Mamo's one and only visit to Rhode Island she showed me how to thread my Singer. I did not progress beyond threading, nor did Mamo's recollection extend to stitching. The only one in the immediate family who can barely claim current use of a sewing machine is my father, retired jurist, who bought a White at a yard sale. Actually Judge persuaded my mother to make the purchase for him while he sat in the car feigning manly disinterest. The cemeteries are rife with people who knew how to make them hum. The Singer itself has been retired to the attic. Over the well, I placed a jagged slab of veined green marble fallen off the front of a building downtown. On top of the slab a covered glazed bowl from the kilns of Gubbio—where we waited out a sudden, fabulous storm before a lengthy, fabulous supper—filled with cotton balls. Also on the marble, an array of shapely jars and bottles containing clarifying lotion, moisturizer, emollient, eaus de toilette. Propped against the wall behind them, a tin mirror from Mexico. I perform my ablutions there. Of a morning and an evening, I face myself, a poet of forty. Within the limits of this diminutive wooden world, I have made do with the cracks of light and tokens of loss and recovery that came my way. I can offer no more explicit demonstration as to what my poetry is. The box this comes in is mine; I remain faithfully, CD.

Born and raised in the Ozarks of Arkansas, C. D. Wright is the author of numerous essays and five previous books of poetry, including *Translations of the Gospel Back into Tongues* and *Further Adventures with You*. She has published her poems in *BRICK, Sulfur, Ironwood, Kenyon Review, Paris Review, Tri-Quarterly,* and *The New Yorker*. She is most recently the recipient of the Whiting Award for Writers and the Governor's Award for the Arts given by the state of Rhode Island, where she now makes her home.

The Contemporary Poetry Series

EDITED BY PAUL ZIMMER

Dannie Abse, *One-Legged on Ice*
Susan Astor, *Dame*
Gerald Barrax, *An Audience of One*
Tony Connor, *New and Selected Poems*
Franz Douskey, *Rowing Across the Dark*
Lynn Emanuel, *Hotel Fiesta*
John Engels, *Vivaldi in Early Fall*
John Engels, *Weather-Fear: New and Selected Poems, 1958–1982*
Brendan Galvin, *Atlantic Flyway*
Brendan Galvin, *Winter Oysters*
Michael Heffernan, *The Cry of Oliver Hardy*
Michael Heffernan, *To the Wreakers of Havoc*
Conrad Hilberry, *The Moon Seen as a Slice of Pineapple*
X. J. Kennedy, *Cross Ties*
Caroline Knox, *The House Party*
Gary Margolis, *The Day We Still Stand Here*
Michael Pettit, *American Light*
Bin Ramke, *White Monkeys*
J. W. Rivers, *Proud and on My Feet*
Laurie Sheck, *Amaranth*
Myra Sklarew, *The Science of Goodbyes*
Marcia Southwick, *The Night Won't Save Anyone*
Mary Swander, *Succession*
Bruce Weigl, *The Monkey Wars*
Paul Zarzyski, *The Make-Up of Ice*

The Contemporary Poetry Series

EDITED BY BIN RAMKE

J. T. Barbarese, *New Science*
J. T. Barbarese, *Under the Blue Moon*
Scott Cairns, *The Translation of Babel*
Richard Cole, *The Glass Children*
Wayne Dodd, *Echoes of the Unspoken*
Wayne Dodd, *Sometimes Music Rises*
Joseph Duemer, *Customs*
Karen Fish, *The Cedar Canoe*
Albert Goldbarth, *Heaven and Earth: A Cosmology*
Caroline Knox, *To Newfoundland*
Patrick Lawler, *A Drowning Man Is Never Tall Enough*
Sydney Lea, *No Sign*
Jeanne Lebow, *The Outlaw James Copeland and the Champion-Belted Empress*
Phillis Levin, *Temples and Fields*
Gary Margolis, *Falling Awake*
Jacqueline Osherow, *Looking for Angels in New York*
Donald Revell, *The Gaza of Winter*
Martha Clare Ronk, *Desire in L.A.*
Aleda Shirley, *Chinese Architecture*
Susan Stewart, *The Hive*
Terese Svoboda, *All Aberration*
Arthur Vogelsang, *Twentieth Century Women*
Sidney Wade, *Empty Sleeves*
C. D. Wright, *String Light*